Whiskey & Wildflowers

Brianne Reilly

BookLeaf Publishing

India | USA | UK

Presentation by *BookLeaf Publishing*

Web: www.bookleafpub.com

E-mail: info@bookleafpub.com

ISBN: 9789363317512

First edition 2024

ACKNOWLEDGMENTS

To those who believed in me,
before I even believed in myself.

<u>*Author's Note*</u>

Dear Reader,

Thank you for embarking on this journey with me.

It's been a long time coming.

Micro poetry holds a special place in my heart, allowing me to explore many themes and feelings in just a few words.

I hope that as you read, you find connections to your own experiences and emotions, just as I did while writing these poems. I look forward to continuing this journey with you in the works to come.

Sincerely,
Brianne Reilly

LOVING SOMEONE

come,
lie naked with me

skin to skin
heart to heart
soul to soul

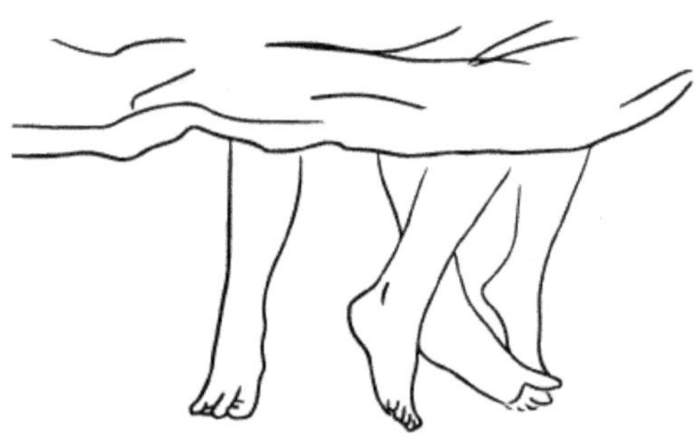

today,
i lay my armor down

for,
you have become my shield

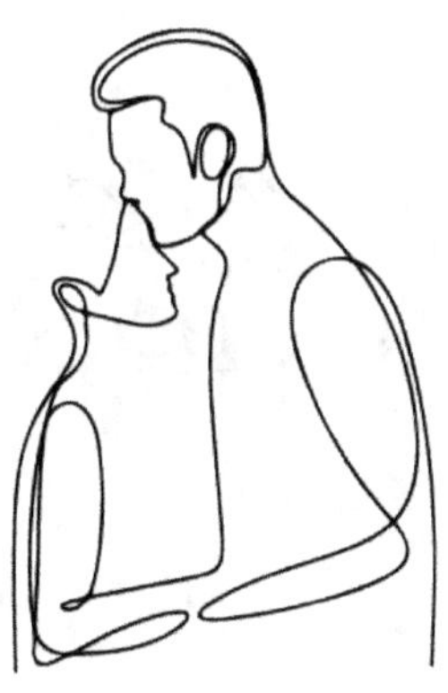

climb the mountain to my heart
cross the valley to my soul
tread the river to my body

do not look for me in the stars

look for me in your heart

for,
that is where i reside

root me in your heart,
as our bodies bloom as one

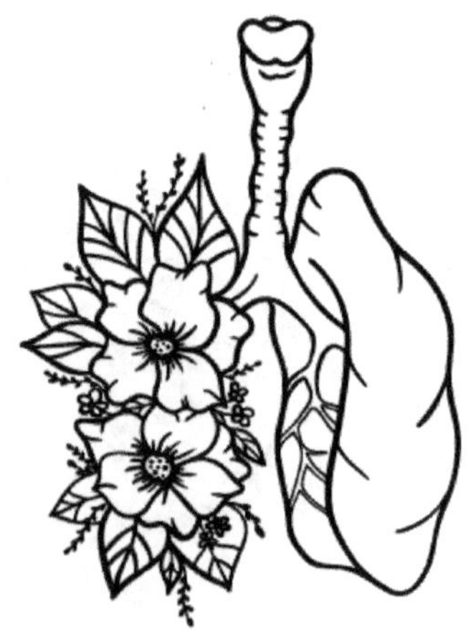

the heat of my thighs buckle under the cool
touch of your palms

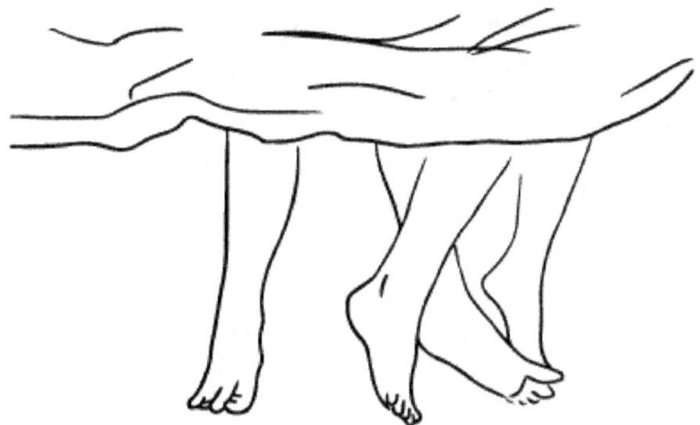

whiskey kisses in leather and lace

i want to undress you

mind
body
soul

your body is the match
mine is the strike

together,
we are the flame

wait for me on the other side of forever

erase these scars on my heart,
write our love story in their place

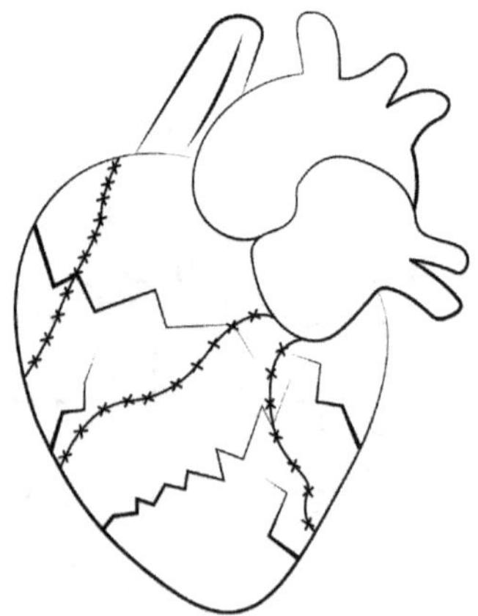

the champagne gold of your skin calls my name

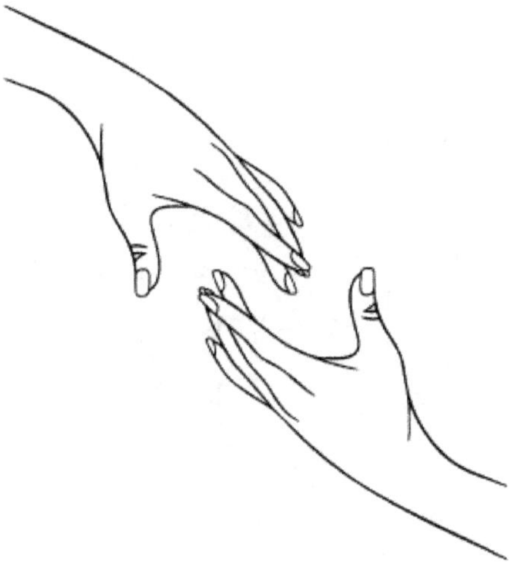

write me a love letter with your tongue

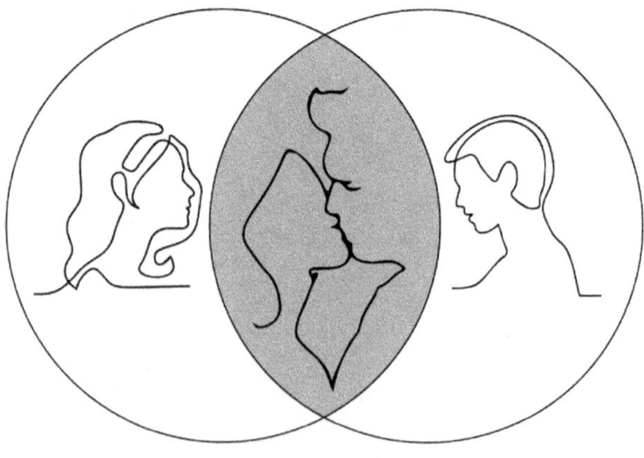

walk with me under the sky
and
we will dance among the stars

i asked him to speak of love
and
he spoke my name

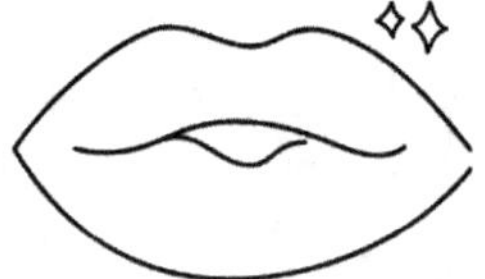

do not navigate oceans for me,
be the wind that guides my sails

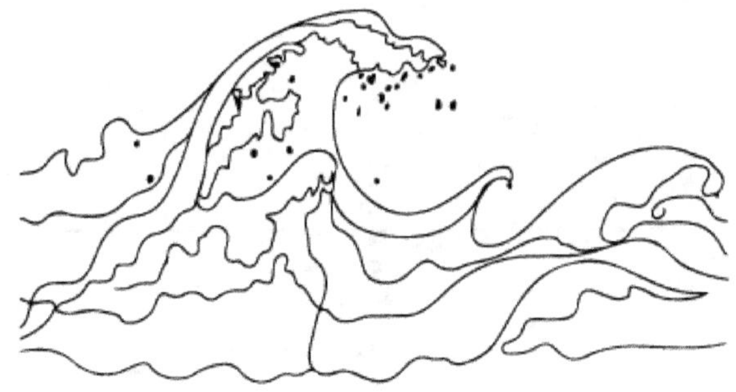

be with me

as still as the *Ocean*
as high as the *Sky*
as grounded as the *Earth*

18

spread my legs,
feast on my hunger

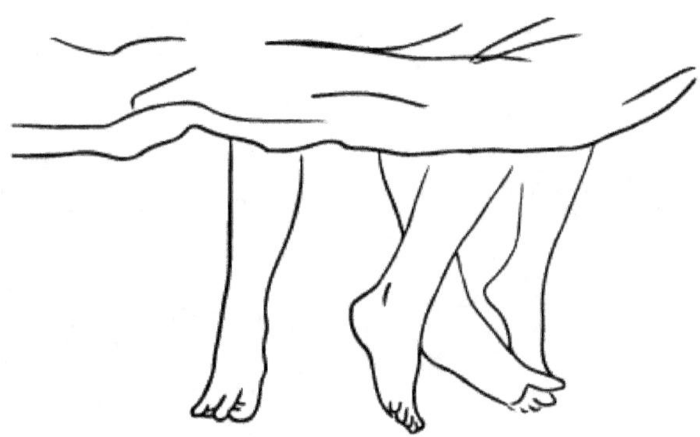

use my body as your map,
lead me to new destinations

your love is the music to which my soul dances

glances pass like time between us

slow and steady,
as we wait for the clock to strike midnight

let's escape down the rabbit hole
let's see what adventures await us

push through our release

take me
as i
take you

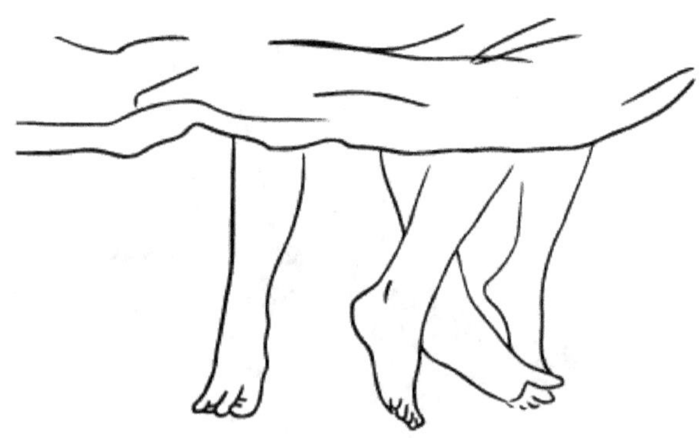

let's get drunk on whiskey, love and bad
decisions

kiss me in my Sunday dress,

embrace my sun-kissed skin as whiskey soaks
my lips

my first love comes in the form of liquid gold
encased in a bottle of green glass

paint me a picture
your body is the brush
mine is the canvas

BREAKING DOWN

the ruins of this house hold

memories once made
promises once spoken

the ruins of this house hold

memories now faded
promises now broken

the asylum at the end of the road is encased in
the screams of patients passed

i heed the call of its dead,
as the debauchery of lost souls lead me home

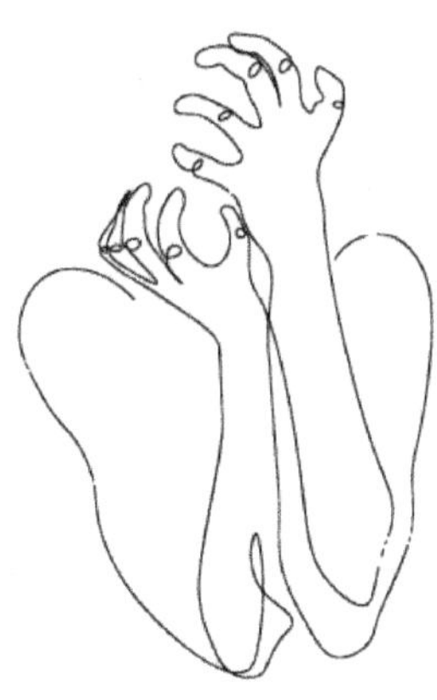

you shiver,

"cold?" i ask
"lonely" you answer

postmarked letters tucked away,
holding words meant to be read

yet,
carrying no hope of delivery

the less i am myself,
the better

the better

for me
for you
for us

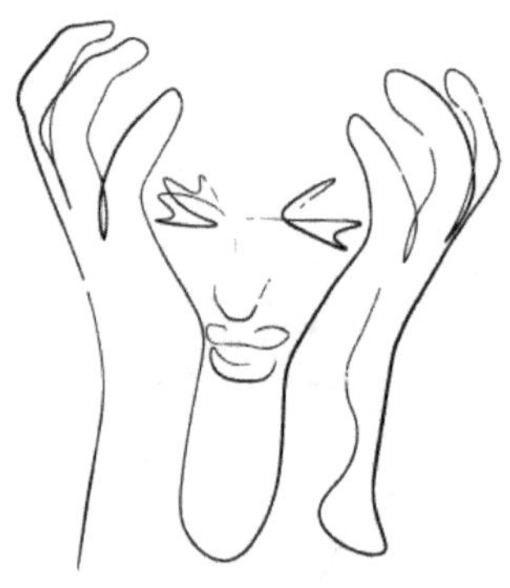

if it's not the same for you
and
it's not the same for me

were we ever really us?

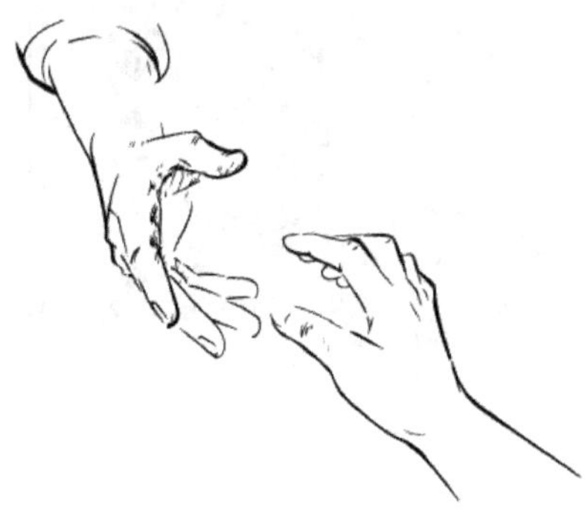

in the end,
we are all a passing fad

the very one you left behind,
is the very one someone else is looking for

my body could not hold my tears

so,
i drown in them

open windows usher in the Autumn breeze,
as i lie here wrapped in thoughts of you

heroin GODS
cocaine GODDESSES
drugged DEVILS
fallen ANGELS

no sober end in sight

was it worth losing yourself in that lie you called
love?

remorse is the disease,
HELL is the hospital

my broken wings sit upon my shattered soul,
resting from a flight never meant to land

it is not from my heart that i write,
but from my soul

how can i write from a heart that is shattered?

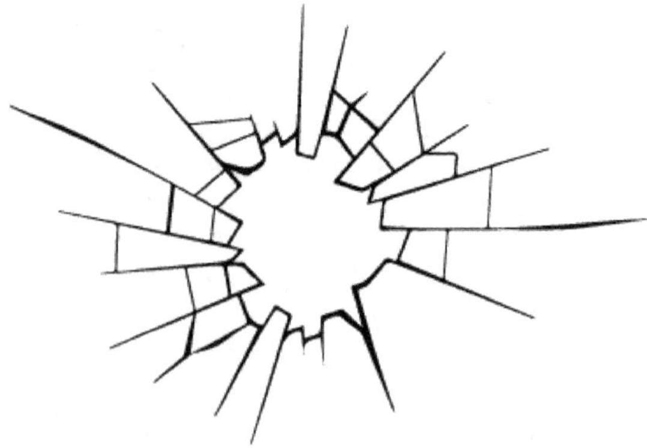

i found the DEVIL in the bottle one night,
he took my hand and led me home

the sharp edges of your heart glide across mine

be careful,
they crave blood

do not travel through my mind

for you will become

as lost as Alice
as mad as the Hatter

the scars on my heart run deeper than those on
my skin

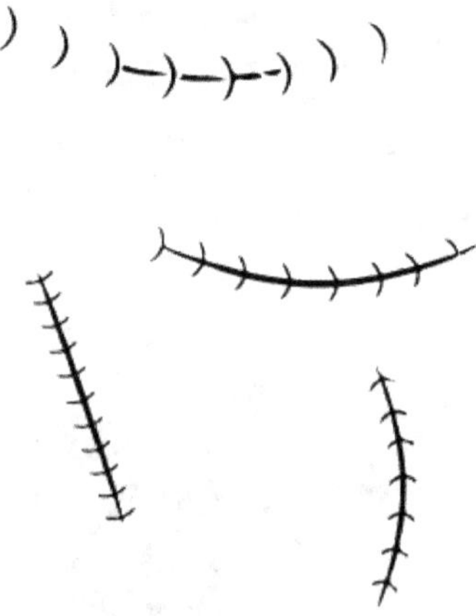

i am filled with a desire for

places i'll never go
people i'll never meet
experiences i'll never have

a life i'll never live

i feel empty inside,
like the hollow chamber of a gun

only,
i never fired my last shot

do not eat the apple,
for you will choke on the sins of others

i lock my heart

not for my protection,
but for yours

you were a wrong turn on this highway i call my
heart

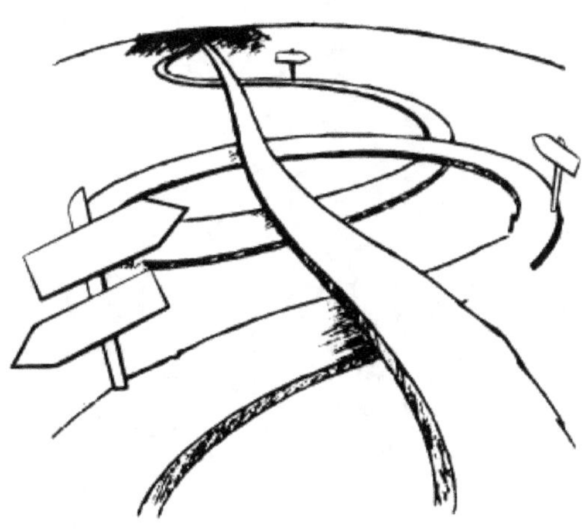

53

this burning house reminds me of our love

first,
we were dancing in the flames

next,
we were buried in the ashes

words are weapons

use them wisely,
for they wield a sword no shield can block

choose your battles wisely,
for some are already lost

come,

we will partake in the DEVIL'S poison as we
dance in the flames of HELL

don't let yourself be collateral damage in
someone else's war against themselves

my tears fall like

Fall leaves
Winter snow
Spring buds
Summer rain

my wounds do not heal,
they simply fade into memories i wish to forget

we are

born out of *chaos*
living in *conflict*
dying of *carelessness*

choose wisely

for,
the DEVIL waits for no man

do not put yourself on loan for those who do not
wish to repay their debts

HEALING

i am healing from wounds you cannot see

please,
be gentle with me

i have found you in my darkest hour,
so that we may walk into the light together

they say words cut like a knife

luckily,
i know how to sew

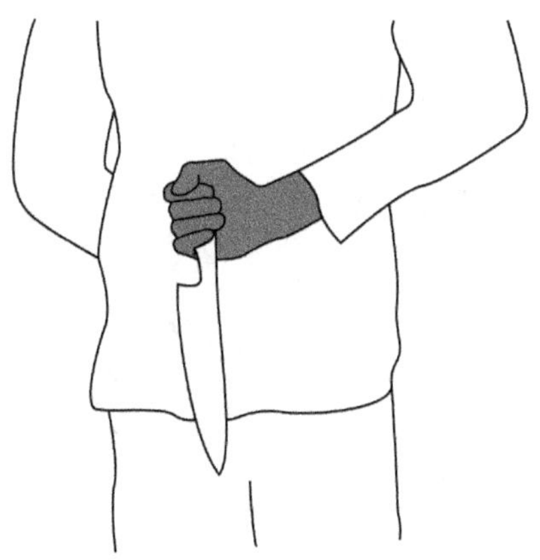

etch these words upon my skin,
so that i may feel them in my soul

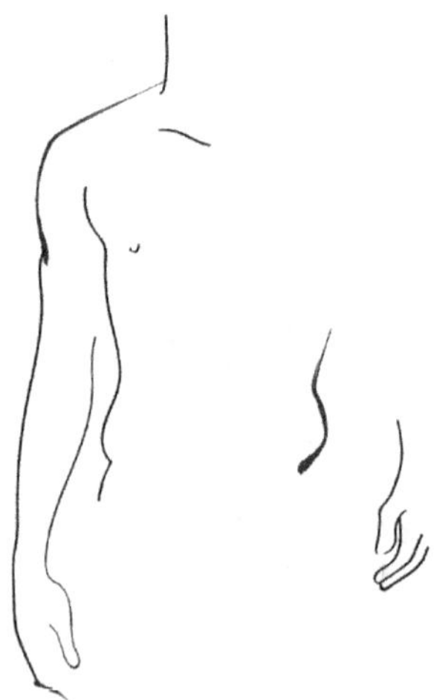

you never need to apologize for how you survive
trauma

it is yours to carry
yours to let go of

when
why
and
how

you choose to survive is yours and yours alone

these mountains are no longer yours to carry
alone

come,
let us divide them in two

one for me
and
one for you

together,
we will reach your destination

thank you for letting me go, because of this i
found
i am better for it

better for me
better for you
better for the illusion of us

i wonder,

if i were to meet you today

would i still say,
"hello?"

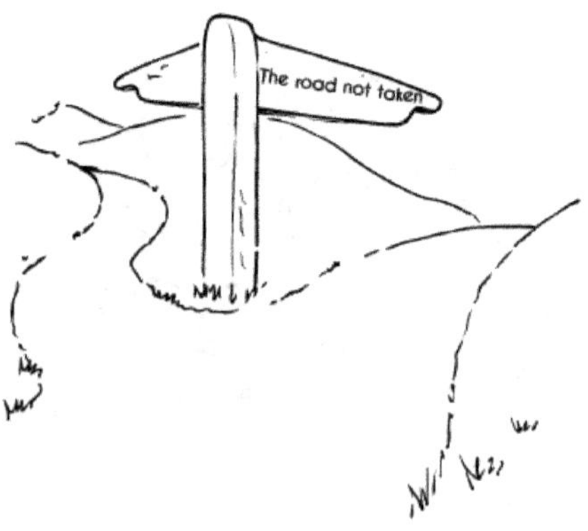

life is like Russian roulette,
the last shot is the deadliest

not because you die

rather because,
you begin again

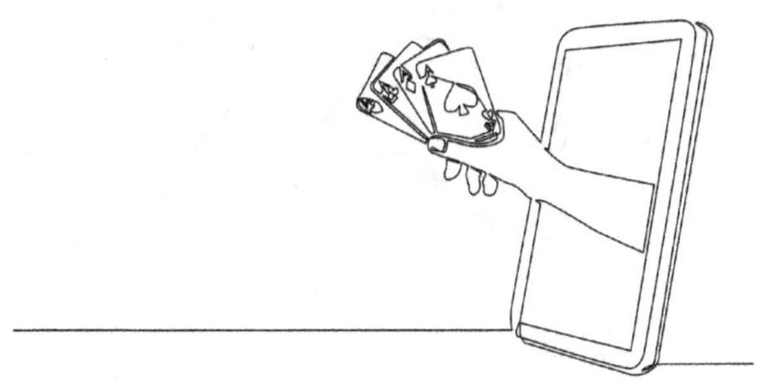

in order to love you,
i must let you go

in order to love me,
i must leave you

in order to love at all,
i must travel alone

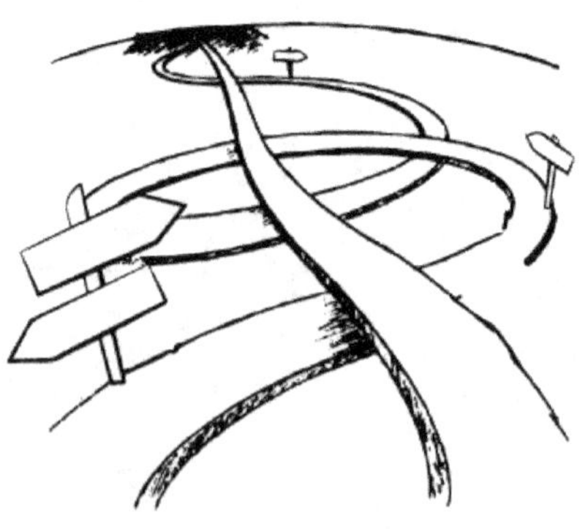